SKILLET

SKILLET

Recipes by Anna Helm Baxter
Photography by Beatriz Da Costa

hardie grant books

CONTENTS

Before having children, I had little understanding of what being stretched for time actually meant. Five years into being a mother, I often find myself asking fellow parents how they manage to get dinner on the table each night. In between homework, putting plasters on boo boos, unpacking and repacking snacks and lunches, bedtime stories and playing tea parties, sometimes it seems the only way to make dinner is by sacrificing family time.

In approaching this book, I wanted to be certain that these recipes were achievable on a weeknight. Achievable after a long day at work. Achievable when you have little humans nipping impatiently at your heels. Achievable at the weekends when you crave something a little more special, but don't want to spend the entire day in the kitchen. Achievable when you don't have a dishwasher (human or machine). There are no hard-to-find ingredients or lengthy directions in these recipes. What you will find are easy, flavourful, complete meals to share with your loved ones. Because really, that's the most important part of going to the effort of making dinner.

WHAT YOU'LL NEED

If a recipe calls for a large skillet, use either a cast iron or clad stainless-steel skillet. The best ones are large, clad stainless-steel skillets with aluminium or copper cores (30–33 cm/12–13 in surface area); large, cast-iron seasoned skillets (30–33 cm/12–13 in surface area) and 23 cm (9 in) cast-iron skillets for baking (see pages 8–9 for more information).

EQUIPMENT

CAST IRON

Cast-iron skillets are more versatile than non-stick ones, and more affordable than clad stainless steel. Sure, they are heavier and require a little more care, but the pros far outweigh the cons. Unlike non-stick pans, cast-iron skillets can be used on all surfaces, including under a hot grill (broiler). They have the ability to retain heat, making them ideal for browning, searing and shallow-frying. They do take time to heat up and can't be left soaking in the sink but if you take care of them they will last a lifetime.

WHAT TO LOOK FOR

A pre-seasoned pan, so your pan is non-stick from the get-go.
High, straight sides, which are good for everything, from braises and stir-fries to baked goods.

DO:

USE on the hob, in the oven, on the barbecue and under the grill (broiler).
USE oven gloves.
WIPE the pan clean with paper towel while still warm.
RUN a dirty pan under hot water.
GENTLY clean with a small amount of soap using a non-abrasive brush or pad.
ALWAYS dry the pan after washing and coat in vegetable oil.
GENTLY heat vegetable oil or lightly rub with coarse salt to remove stubborn food residue.
KEEP a second pan for cooking seafood.

DON'T:

SOAK in the sink or store wet.
SLOW COOK acidic foods, such as tomato sauce.
USE lots of soap or abrasive cleaning pads.

TRADITIONAL SKILLET

Clad stainless steel is a great multi-purpose choice, but always look for a pan that's tri-ply or 'clad' with an aluminium or copper core. Clad stainless steel is versatile, non-reactive to acidic foods and, when properly pre-heated, food shouldn't stick to the surface. Brown spots may form over time but these can be scrubbed away.

DO:

LOOK for a pan with an oven-safe handle.
USE on the hob, in the oven, on the barbecue and under the grill (broiler).
HEAT your pan and do the water test (see opposite) to check for readiness.
SOAK pans in warm, soapy water or gently boil water in the pan before scrubbing.
LET the pan cool before cleaning.

DON'T:

TRY to force food to flip.
TRY to cook over high heat, which leads to food sticking and burning.

THE WATER TEST

A common mistake with stainless steel is to not give the pan enough time to heat up before starting to cook. This will almost guarantee that your food will stick to the surface of the pan and not release easily. A great way to test if your stainless-steel pan is hot enough is to use the water test.

Heat the pan over medium—high heat. Add ⅛ teaspoon water and watch it sit before gradually bubbling away.

Add another ⅛ teaspoon water and it should break into droplets that dance round the pan.

Repeat until the water forms a single ball that rolls around the pan. At this point, it has reached the perfect temperature to add oil and begin cooking. Adjust the temperature to avoid any overheating as necessary.

SKILLET

SPANAKOPITA PIE

SERVES 6

2 tablespoons olive oil
1 large onion, chopped
900 g (2 lb) frozen chopped spinach, thawed
4 large eggs, lightly beaten
350 g (12 oz) whole milk ricotta
125 g (4 oz) feta, crumbled
7 sheets filo pastry
25 g (1 oz) unsalted butter, melted
1 tablespoon sesame seeds

Preheat the oven to 190°C (375°F/ Gas 5). Heat a large cast-iron skillet over medium heat, add the oil and fry the onion until tender. Remove from the heat. Squeeze any excess liquid from the spinach and mix with the onion. Stir in the eggs and cheeses. Working one sheet at a time, brush the filo with butter, scrunch it up and arrange on top of the spinach in a single layer. Sprinkle with sesame seeds and bake for 25–30 minutes until golden.

SHALLOT & BLUE CHEESE PIE

SERVES 4

1 tablespoon olive oil
105 g (3½ oz) very cold unsalted butter, cubed
350 g (12 oz) medium—small shallots, halved, roots trimmed
sea salt and freshly ground black pepper
1 teaspoon thyme leaves
250 g (9 oz/1⅔ cup) plain (all-purpose) flour
2 teaspoons baking powder
150 g (5 oz) crumbled blue cheese
75 ml (2½ fl oz) whole milk
2 large eggs

Preheat the oven to 200°C (400°F/ Gas 6). Heat a 23 cm (9 in) cast-iron skillet over medium heat, add the oil and 1 tablespoon butter. Once the butter is foaming, reduce the heat and fry the shallots, cut sides down, until golden. Turn and cook until tender. Remove from the heat, season and sprinkle over the thyme. Mix the flour, baking powder and ½ teaspoon salt in a bowl. Rub the remaining butter into the flour mixure, then fold in 100 g (3½ oz) blue cheese. Whisk the milk and eggs together, then use a fork to fold the wet ingredients into the dry to make a dough. Sprinkle the remaining cheese over the shallots and press the dough on top. Bake for 23—26 minutes. Rest for 5 minutes, then invert onto a plate to serve.

BEETROOT TARTE TATIN

SERVES 4

10 g (½ oz) unsalted butter
530 g (1 lb 3 oz) small beetroot, trimmed,
  peeled and halved
1 tablespoon brown sugar
1 tablespoon apple-cider vinegar
300 g (10½ oz) pre-rolled puff pastry
75 g (2½ oz) herbed goat's cheese
handful of mint leaves
15 g (½ oz) shelled unsalted pistachios,
  roughly chopped

Preheat the oven to 200°C (400°F/
Gas 6). Heat a 23 cm (9 in) cast-
iron skillet over medium heat, add
the butter, then the beetroot, cut
side down. After 2 minutes, sprinkle
over the sugar and vinegar. Simmer
for 2 minutes until slightly
caramelised. Cover with foil and
bake for 20 minutes until tender.
Remove from the oven and increase
the heat to 220°C (425°F/Gas 7).
Cut out a 23 cm (9 in) round of
puff pastry and lay over the top,
pushing down. Bake for 20 minutes,
or until puffed and golden. Invert
and dot with cheese, mint and nuts.

KALE & AGED GOUDA STRATA

SERVES 6—8

2 tablespoons olive oil
1 red onion, diced
200 g (7 oz) kale, thick stems removed, leaves chopped
8 large eggs
700 ml (23½ fl oz/3 cups) whole milk
1 tablespoon Dijon mustard
300 g (10½ oz) day-old rustic bread, cut into cubes
150 g (5 oz) aged Gouda or extra-mature Cheddar, grated
sea salt and freshly ground black pepper

Heat a large cast-iron skillet over medium heat, add 1 tablespoon oil and fry the onion, covered, for 10 minutes. Uncover and cook until golden. Remove from the skillet and wipe out. Return the skillet to the heat and add the remaining oil, kale and 2 tablespoons water. Cover and wilt for 3—4 minutes. Remove from the skillet; wipe clean. Beat the eggs, milk, Dijon mustard and onion in a bowl and season with ½ teaspoon each of salt and pepper. Scatter the bottom of the skillet with a layer of bread, then kale and half the cheese, then repeat. Pour over the egg mixture and chill for 8—24 hours. Preheat the oven to 180°C (350°F/Gas 4). Bake for 45—50 minutes until set.

EGGS & GREENS

SERVES 2

3 tablespoons olive oil
3 large garlic cloves, thinly sliced
750 g (1 lb 10 oz) rainbow chard, stems finely chopped,
   leaves roughly chopped
3 anchovies
sea salt and freshly ground black pepper
juice and grated zest of **1** lemon
25 g (1 oz) Parmesan, finely grated
4 large eggs

Preheat the oven to 150°C (300°F/Gas 2). Heat
a large cast-iron skillet over medium heat, add
2 tablespoons oil and fry the garlic for
2 minutes. Remove the garlic from the pan,
reduce the heat to medium—low and add the chard
stems and anchovies. Season and cook, covered,
until softened. Add the remaining oil and chard
leaves, tossing until barely wilted. Remove
the pan from the heat. Drain any liquid in the
base of the pan and add the lemon juice, zest
and cheese. Make four wells in the greens and
crack the eggs inside. Bake for 10—12 minutes,
covering after 8 minutes, until the whites are
set. Scatter over the garlic and season.

MUSHROOM, LEEK & RICOTTA FRITTATA

SERVES 4

3–4 tablespoons olive oil
2 thin leeks, white and light green parts
   sliced into half moons
800 g (1 lb 12 oz) wild mushrooms, tough
   stems discarded, caps roughly torn
sea salt and freshly ground black pepper
10 large eggs
25 g (1 oz) grated Parmesan
125 g (4 oz) whole milk ricotta

Heat the grill (broiler) to high. Heat
a large skillet over medium heat, add
3 tablespoons oil then fry the leeks,
mushrooms and ¼ teaspoon each of salt
and pepper for 10–12 minutes until
softened, adding extra oil if
necessary. In a bowl, lightly beat
the eggs with the Parmesan and a pinch
each of salt and pepper. Add to the
pan, stirring, and cook for 1 minute,
then dot with ricotta. Grill for
1–3 minutes until just set.

SPINACH & ARTICHOKE PIZZA

SERVES 4

4 teaspoons olive oil
2 garlic cloves, finely chopped
150 g (5 oz) baby spinach, thick stems discarded
200 g (7 oz) whole milk ricotta
35 g (1¼ oz) Parmesan, finely grated
100 g (3½ oz) frozen baby artichokes, roughly chopped
sea salt and freshly ground black pepper
70 g (2½ oz) grated mozzarella
450 g (1 lb) fresh pizza dough

Preheat the oven to 260°C (500°F/Gas 10) and place an oven rack in the lower third of the oven. Heat a large, cast-iron skillet over medium heat, add 2 teaspoons oil and fry the garlic for 1 minute. Add the spinach and cook until just wilted. Remove from the pan, pat dry with paper towel, then chop. Wipe the pan. Combine the ricotta, Parmesan and artichokes. Season, then fold in the spinach mixture and 30 g (1 oz) mozzarella. Press the pizza dough into the skillet, then top with the ricotta mixture, sprinkle with the remaining mozzarella and bake until puffed and golden.

SPANISH SWEET POTATO TORTILLA

SERVES 6

130 ml (4½ fl oz) olive oil
750 g (1 lb 10 oz) sweet potatoes (approx. **2** large),
  peeled, halved and cut into 5 mm (¼ in) slices
10 large eggs, lightly beaten
sea salt and freshly ground black pepper
1 onion, sliced
50 g (2 oz) Manchego, grated

Heat 100 ml (3½ fl oz) oil in a large cast-iron
skillet and fry the potatoes for 25–30 minutes,
turning occasionally, until tender but not
brown. Remove from the pan. Beat the eggs with
¾ teaspoon salt and ¼ teaspoon pepper. Fry the
onion for 10 minutes until tender. Heat the
grill (broiler) to high. Add the potatoes and
onions to the eggs. Drain the excess oil from
the pan and wipe clean. Add the remaining oil
and the egg mixture, gently stirring for
1 minute. Cook for another minute without
stirring. Sprinkle with the cheese and grill
for 3–4 minutes until set.

ROASTED SQUASH PANZANELLA

SERVES 4

200 g (7 oz) day-old rustic bread, torn into chunks
4 tablespoons olive oil
25 g (1 oz) Parmesan, finely grated
sea salt and freshly ground black pepper
500 g (1 lb 2 oz) butternut squash, peeled, seeded and
   cut into 5 cm (2 in) cubes
1 red onion, cut into wedges
200 g (7 oz) baby kale
4 tablespoons tahini
4 tablespoons lemon juice
40 g (1½ oz) pomegranate seeds

Preheat the oven to 220°C (430°F/Gas 7). Toss
the bread with 2 tablespoons oil and the
Parmesan in a large cast-iron skillet. Season
with salt and pepper. Bake for 8–10 minutes
until golden brown; remove from the pan. Toss
the squash and onion in the remaining oil in
the pan. Season and cook in the oven for
20–25 minutes, until golden, tossing halfway
through. Fold in the kale and croutons. Combine
the tahini, lemon juice and 4 tablespoons
water, season and toss with the squash mixture.
Sprinkle with pomegranate seeds.

CAULIFLOWER FRIED RICE

SERVES 4

½ large head cauliflower (about **750 g/1 lb 10 oz**), cut into florets, tough stems discarded
2 tablespoons coconut or vegetable oil
1 red (bell) pepper, cut into small pieces
2 spring onions (scallions), thinly sliced
20 g (¾ oz) piece of ginger, peeled and cut into thin matchsticks
3 tablespoons soy sauce
2 teaspoons chilli paste
2 teaspoons honey
4 large eggs, lightly beaten
150 g (5 oz) frozen peas, thawed

Pulse the cauliflower in batches in a food processor until it resembles rice. Heat a large cast-iron skillet over medium—high heat. Add 1 tablespoon oil, then stir-fry the pepper, white parts of the spring onion and the ginger for 2 minutes. Add the cauliflower, toss and cook, covered, for 5 minutes, stirring once. Whisk the soy sauce, chilli paste and honey together. Push the cauliflower mix to one side of the pan, add the remaining oil, then the eggs, scrambling until cooked. Remove from the heat; fold in the eggs, sauce and peas. Serve with the spring onion greens.

CHICKPEA & HERB PILAF

SERVES 4

2 courgettes (zucchini), cut into half
  moons
sea salt and freshly ground black pepper**3
  tablespoons** olive oil
1 red onion, chopped
300 g (10½ oz/1½ cups) basmati rice, rinsed
750 ml (25½ fl oz/3 cups) vegetable stock
50 g (2 oz) raisins
1 x 400 g (14 oz) tin chickpeas
  (garbanzos), drained and rinsed
4 tablespoons finely chopped dill
35 g (1 oz) pine nuts

Season the courgettes. Heat a large
skillet over medium—high heat. Add
2 tablespoons oil and fry the
courgettes until starting to
soften. Remove from the pan. Reduce
the heat to medium—low, add the
remaining oil and cook the onion
for 8—10 minutes until very tender.
Add the rice and stir to coat. Add
the stock and raisins, cover and
simmer for 15—20 minutes until the
rice is tender, stirring every
5 minutes. Fold in the chickpeas
and dill. Top with the courgettes
and pine nuts.

HUEVOS RANCHEROS

SERVES 4

5 tablespoons vegetable oil
1 large garlic clove, roughly chopped
1 x 400 g (14 oz) tin black beans, rinsed
750 g (1 lb 10 oz) tomatoes, chopped
sea salt and freshly ground black pepper
8 corn tortillas
4 large eggs
15 g (½ oz) coriander (cilantro) leaves
100 g (3½ oz) feta, crumbled

Heat a large skillet over medium—high heat.
Add 1 tablespoon oil and fry the garlic until
starting to turn golden. Add the beans and toss
to warm through. Add the tomatoes, season,
toss, then transfer the salsa to a bowl and
keep warm. Wipe out the pan. Heat the remaining
oil and warm the tortillas in batches for
1—2 minutes per side until golden. Transfer to
a plate and cover. Crack the eggs into the hot
oil and fry, sunny side up, until cooked to
your liking. Serve with the tortillas, salsa,
coriander and feta.

FRIED RICOTTA DUMPLINGS

SERVES 4

450 g (1 lb) whole milk ricotta
50 g (2 oz) Parmesan, finely grated
1 large egg
20 g (¾ oz) basil leaves, half chopped, smaller
  leaves reserved
freshly ground black pepper
130 g (4½ oz) plain (all-purpose) flour, plus extra
  for dusting
3 tablespoons olive oil, plus extra to serve
4 tablespoons capers, rinsed and patted dry
3 garlic cloves, finely chopped

Combine both cheeses, the egg, chopped basil
and ½ teaspoon pepper in a bowl. Sift over
65 g (2¼ oz) flour and gently mix. Transfer to
a floured surface, sift over the remaining flour
and knead to make a soft dough. Divide into
four pieces and roll each piece into a long
rope about 2 cm (¾ in) thick. Cut into 3 cm
(1¼ in) pieces and transfer to a parchment
paper-lined baking sheet. Freeze for at least
4 hours until solid. Heat a large cast-iron
skillet over medium heat, add 1 tablespoon oil
and cook the capers and garlic until light
golden brown. Scrape into the bowl. Return the
pan to the heat. Working in two batches, heat
1 tablespoon oil at a time and cook the frozen
dumplings for 2 minutes per side until golden
brown. Top with the caper mixture, reserved
basil and drizzle with oil.

PARMESAN RISOTTO

SERVES 4

60 g (2 oz) unsalted butter
1 onion, finely chopped
300 g (10½ oz) arborio rice
150 ml (5 fl oz) dry white wine
1.2 litres (41 fl oz) hot vegetable stock
75 g (2½ oz) Parmesan, finely grated, plus extra to serve
sea salt and freshly ground black pepper
1 small handful of flat-leaf parsley, chopped

Heat a large skillet over medium heat, add
35 g (1¼ oz) butter and fry the onion for
10—12 minutes until very tender. Add the rice,
stirring to coat, then add the wine and bring
to a simmer. Add half of the stock and simmer
for 5 minutes. Add the remaining stock and
simmer for 12 minutes until the rice is
cooked. Remove from the heat and fold in
the cheese and remaining butter. Season and
sprinkle with parsley.

ROASTED CARROT & COUSCOUS SALAD

SERVES 4

1 red onion, cut into thin wedges
2 tablespoons olive oil
sea salt and freshly ground black pepper
450 g (1 lb) rainbow carrots, cut into 6 cm
  (2½ in) long pieces (halve thicker ends)
200 g (7 oz) couscous
2 tablespoons lemon juice
100 g (3½ oz) feta
15 g (½ oz) flat-leaf parsley, leaves
  roughly chopped
50 g (2 oz) toasted hazelnuts, roughly
  chopped
1 avocado, peeled, stoned and sliced

Preheat the oven to 190°C (375°F/
Gas 5). Toss the onion with
1 tablespoon oil in a large
skillet, season and roast for
20 minutes. Add the carrots and
roast for 20—25 minutes until
tender. Pour 350 ml (12 fl oz)
just-boiled water over the couscous,
cover and leave for 10 minutes.
Fluff with a fork and season. Add the
lemon juice, remaining oil, feta,
parsley, onion and carrots, then
sprinkle with hazelnuts and avocado.

CHILEQUILES

SERVES 4

500 g (1 lb 2 oz) tomatillos or green
  tomatoes, husked and quartered
1 large white onion, cut into 8 pieces
6 garlic cloves
2 jalapeño chillies, thinly sliced
1 large bunch of coriander (cilantro),
  half roughly chopped (including stems),
  half leaves picked
225 g (8 oz) tortilla chips
100 g (3½ oz) Monterey jack or mature
  Cheddar, grated
4 radishes, very thinly sliced
1 avocado, peeled, stoned and cut into
  small pieces
2 tablespoons lime juice (about **1** lime)

Preheat the oven to 220°C (430°F/
Gas 7). Heat a large skillet over
medium—high heat and cook the
tomatillos, onion, garlic and
1 chilli for 10 minutes, shaking
the pan occasionally, until charred
and softened. Transfer to a food
processor and pulse until smooth.
Add the chopped coriander and pulse
to combine. Return the tomatillo
mix to pan with 125 ml (4 fl oz/
½ cup) water and simmer for
5 minutes. Add the tortilla chips
and turn to coat. Sprinkle over the
cheese and bake for 12—15 minutes
until bubbling. Toss the remaining
chilli in a bowl with the coriander
leaves, radishes, avocado and lime
juice. Spoon over the chilequiles.

SKILLET

FISH &
SEAFOOD

ROASTED COD & PATATAS BRAVAS

SERVES 4

650 g (1 lb 7 oz) potatoes, peeled and cut
    into 2.5 cm (1 in) pieces
1 red (bell) pepper, seeded and cut
    into 1 cm (½ in) pieces
2 tablespoons olive oil
1½ teaspoons smoked paprika
1 lemon, sliced, plus **1 tablespoon**
    lemon juice
sea salt and freshly ground black pepper
500 g (1 lb 2 oz) skinless cod, cut into
    4 fillets, patted dry
75 g (2½ oz) mayonnaise
1 garlic clove, very finely chopped

Preheat the oven to 230°C (450°F/
Gas 8) and place an oven rack in
the bottom third of the oven. Heat
a large cast-iron skillet over
medium—high heat. Toss potatoes and
pepper with the oil, 1 teaspoon
paprika and the sliced lemon and
season. Cook for 5 minutes then
roast in the oven for 20—25 minutes
until starting to turn golden,
stirring halfway through. Remove
the lemon if burning. Season the
fish, place on top of the potatoes
and cook for 8—12 minutes until
opaque. Combine the mayonnaise,
remaining paprika, lemon juice and
garlic. Serve with the fish, lemon
slices and potatoes.

MEDITERRANEAN PRAWNS

SERVES 4

3 tablespoons olive oil
2 large yellow (bell) peppers, seeded and cut into 10 cm (4 in) pieces
4 garlic cloves, chopped
4 spring onions (scallions), thinly sliced, whites and greens separated
450 g (1 lb) peeled and deveined prawns (shrimps)
1 x 400 g (14 oz) tin butter beans, drained and rinsed
2 tablespoons white wine
1 tablespoon lemon juice, plus **1 teaspoon** grated zest
100 g (3½ oz) feta

Preheat the oven to 220°C (430°F/Gas 7). Heat a large skillet over medium heat, add 2 tablespoons oil and cook the peppers until starting to soften. Add the garlic and spring onion whites and cook for 1 minute. Remove from the heat. Fold in the prawns, beans, wine, lemon juice, zest and the remaining oil, then season. Top with feta and bake for 12–15 minutes until the prawns are opaque. Sprinkle with spring onion greens.

ISRAELI COUSCOUS PAELLA

SERVES 4–6

60 g (2 oz) Spanish dried chorizo, peeled and diced
2 tablespoons olive oil
450 g (1 lb) mixed de-shelled seafood, such as prawns (shrimps), calamari
   rings and baby scallops, patted dry
sea salt and freshly ground black pepper
1 onion, finely chopped
300 g (10½ oz) Israeli (pearl) couscous
125 ml (4 fl oz/½ cup) dry white wine
1 litre (34 fl oz/4 cups) chicken stock
1 large pinch of saffron threads
2 large tomatoes, peeled and chopped
1 handful of flat-leaf parsley, roughly chopped

Fry the chorizo in a large, dry skillet over medium heat for
5 minutes until crisp. Transfer to a plate lined with kitchen
paper. Add 1 tablespoon oil to the pan, season the shellfish
and fry for 1 minute per side until opaque; transfer to a plate.
Add the remaining oil and cook the onion for 5 minutes until
slightly softened. Add the couscous, stir to coat, then add
the wine and simmer until almost fully absorbed. Add the stock,
saffron and tomatoes and simmer, covered, for 10 minutes.
Uncover, fold in the chorizo and cook for 10 minutes. Fold in
the cooked seafood and juices, and top with parsley.

ROASTED SALMON WITH TOMATOES & GREEN BEANS

SERVES 2

185 g (6½ oz) green beans, trimmed
150 g (5 oz) multicoloured baby plum tomatoes
50 g (2 oz) pitted kalamata olives
4 anchovies
1 tablespoon olive oil
sea salt and freshly ground black pepper
2 x 175 g (6 oz) pieces skinless middle-cut salmon

Preheat the oven to 220°C (430°F/Gas 7). Heat
a large skillet over medium—high heat, add the
beans and 50 ml (2 fl oz) water, cover and cook
for 3 minutes, shaking the pan occasionally.
Drain the beans and transfer to a bowl. Wipe
out the pan. Toss the beans with the tomatoes,
olives, anchovies and oil and season. Return
to the pan and roast for 8 minutes. Season the
salmon and nestle into the pan. Roast for
10—12 minutes until the salmon is opaque.

COCONUT MUSSELS

SERVES 2

1 **tablespoon** coconut oil, melted
20 g (¾ oz) piece of ginger, peeled and julienned
4 spring onions (scallions), thinly sliced, light and dark greens separated
2 large garlic cloves, chopped
1 red chilli, seeded and thinly sliced
1 x 400 ml (13 fl oz) tin coconut milk
grated zest of **1** lime
900 g (2 lb) mussels, scrubbed and debearded
2 tablespoons lime juice (about **1** lime)

Heat a large skillet over medium heat, add the oil, ginger, light parts of the spring onions, garlic and half the chilli and stir-fry for 3 minutes. Add the coconut milk and lime zest, simmer, then add the mussels. Return to a simmer, cover and cook for 4–5 minutes until the mussels open. Discard any unopened mussels. Add the lime juice. Sprinkle with the remaining spring onions and chilli.

SCALLOPS & CHORIZO

SERVES 2

75 g (2½ oz) Spanish dried chorizo, sliced into rounds
250 g (9 oz) small dry bay scallops
75 g (2½ oz) sweetcorn, thawed if frozen
1 tablespoon lime juice, plus lime wedges to serve
1 tablespoon chopped coriander (cilantro) leaves
crusty bread, to serve

Cook the chorizo in a large, dry skillet until crisp. Remove from the pan. Add the scallops and cook in the chorizo oil for 1 minute per side. Return the chorizo to the pan with the corn, add the lime juice and let it bubble. Remove from the heat. Sprinkle with the coriander. Serve with bread and lime wedges.

PRAWN PARMESAN

SERVES 4

4 tablespoons olive oil
180 g (6½ oz) rustic bread, torn into 2 cm
  (¾ in) pieces
2 garlic cloves, finely chopped
450 g (1 lb) colourful tomatoes, cut into
  1 cm (½ in) pieces
sea salt and freshly ground black pepper
1 tablespoon oregano leaves
450 g (1 lb) large peeled and deveined
  prawns (shrimps)
100 g (3½ oz) mozzarella, torn into large
  pieces
50 g (2 oz) Parmesan, finely grated

Preheat the oven to 220°C (430°F/
Gas 7). Heat a large skillet over
medium–low heat. Add 2 tablespoons
oil and the bread and toss to coat.
Season and bake for 8–10 minutes
until golden brown and crisp.
Transfer the bread to a plate,
add the remaining oil and fry the
garlic, stirring, for 1 minute. Add
the tomatoes, season and cook for
3 minutes. Fold in the oregano and
cook for 1 minute. Fold the prawns
and bread into the tomatoes. Top
with the cheeses and bake for
14–16 minutes until golden brown
and bubbling.

EASY FISH PIE

SERVES 6

3 tablespoons olive oil
300 g (10½ oz) mushrooms, sliced
200 g (7 oz) crème fraîche
2 tablespoons finely chopped dill
1 teaspoon grated lemon zest
50 g (2 oz) panko breadcrumbs
50 g (2 oz) Parmesan, finely grated
700 g (1 lb 9 oz) boneless skinless fish, such as salmon,
    smoked haddock or cod
sea salt and freshly ground black pepper

Preheat the oven to 220°C (430°F/Gas 7). Heat a large skillet over medium–high heat. Add 2 tablespoons oil and cook the mushrooms for 6–8 minutes until golden brown and the liquid has evaporated. Remove the pan from the heat. Combine the crème fraîche, dill and lemon zest. In another bowl, combine the panko with the remaining oil, then add the Parmesan. Season the fish and place in a single layer on top of the mushrooms. Pour over the crème fraîche and sprinkle over the breadcrumbs. Bake for 15–20 minutes until the fish is cooked.

SALMON BURGERS

SERVES 4

1 shallot, finely chopped
2 tablespoons red wine vinegar
450 g (1 lb) boneless skinless salmon, cut into large
  chunks
1 spring onion (scallion), finely chopped
sea salt and freshly ground black pepper
1 tablespoon olive oil
3 tablespoons mayonnaise
2 teaspoons sriracha
4 brioche burger buns, lightly toasted
1 small avocado, peeled, stoned and sliced

Combine the shallot and vinegar in a bowl,
tossing occasionally for at least 10 minutes.
Pulse the salmon, spring onion and ¼ teaspoon
each of salt and pepper in a food processor
to small chunks (do not purée). Form into
four thick burgers. Heat a large skillet over
medium—high heat. Add the oil, then fry the
burgers for 3—4 minutes per side until opaque.
Combine the mayonnaise and sriracha and spread
it onto the buns. Top with salmon, avocado
and shallots.

GREEN CURRY & NOODLES

SERVES 4

200 g (7 oz) instant rice noodles
1 **tablespoon** vegetable or coconut oil
1 x 43 g (1½ oz) packet or **3 tablespoons** green curry
   paste
1 x 400 ml (13 fl oz) tin coconut milk
1 **tablespoon** lime juice, plus **2 teaspoons** grated zest
1 **tablespoon** fish sauce
500 g (1 lb 2 oz) skinless boneless fish, such as cod or
   salmon, cut into 3 cm (1¼ in) pieces
100 g (3½ oz) shelled edamame
1 handful of coriander (cilantro) leaves

Cover the noodles with boiling water and leave
to soak according to packet instructions;
drain. Heat a large skillet over medium—high
heat. Add the oil, then the curry paste and
cook, stirring, for 1 minute. Add the coconut
milk, 300 ml (10 fl oz) water, the lime zest
and juice and the fish sauce. Bring to a
simmer, add the fish and edamame and cook for
5 minutes until opaque. Spoon into bowls full
of noodles and top with coriander.

SKILLET

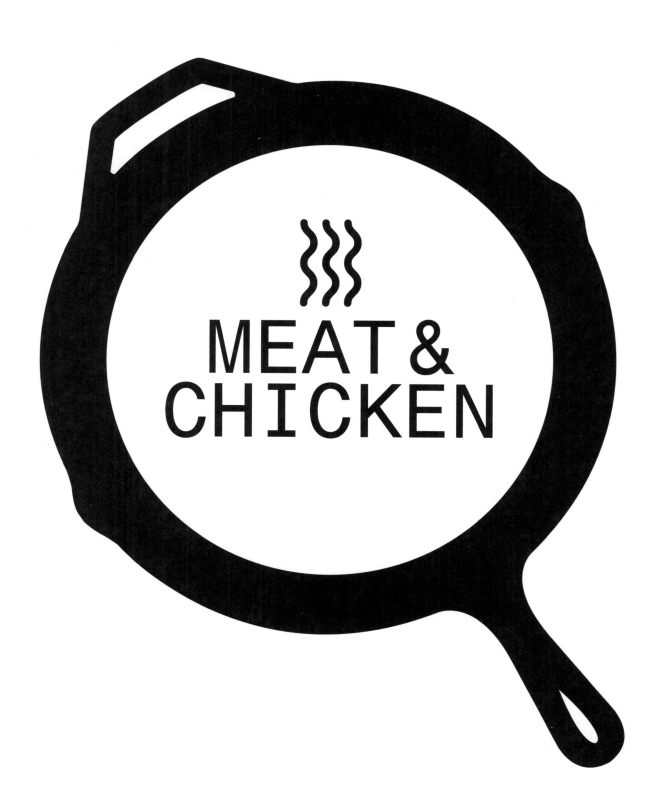

MEAT &
CHICKEN

CHICKEN & MUSHROOM POT PIE

SERVES 4

2 tablespoons olive oil
sea salt and freshly ground black pepper
2 leeks, white and green parts
200 g (7 oz) chestnut mushrooms, sliced
1 rounded tablespoon plain (all-purpose) flour
125 ml (4 fl oz/½ cup) white wine
1.3–1.8kg (2 lb 14 oz–4 lb) rotisserie chicken, skin and
    bones discarded, meat shredded (about **700 g/1 lb 9 oz**
    meat)
350 ml (12 fl oz) chicken stock
50 ml (2 fl oz) double (heavy) cream
225 g (8 oz) pre-rolled shortcrust pastry round

Preheat the oven to 200°C (400°F/Gas 6). Heat
a large skillet over medium heat, add the oil
and cook the leeks and mushrooms until
softened. Sprinkle over the flour and stir to
coat. Add the wine and cook until almost fully
absorbed. Fold in the chicken, then add the
stock and cream. Simmer for 1 minute, then
remove from the heat. Unroll the pastry, place
it on top and cut a small slit in middle. Bake
for 20–25 minutes until golden.

SPRING CHICKEN & ASPARAGUS

SERVES 4

8 small chicken thighs
sea salt and freshly ground black pepper
2 teaspoons olive oil
3 small shallots, peeled and chopped
2 garlic cloves, roughly chopped
125 ml (4 fl oz/½ cup) white wine
125 ml (4 fl oz/½ cup) chicken stock
450 g (1 lb) thin asparagus, tough woody stems trimmed
50 ml (2 fl oz) double (heavy) cream
1 tablespoon chopped tarragon

Season the chicken. Heat a large skillet over medium—high heat. Add the oil and cook the chicken, skin side down, for 7—10 minutes until golden brown and crisp. Turn and cook for another 3 minutes, then remove from the pan. Discard all but 1 tablespoon fat. Add the shallots and garlic and fry for 3 minutes. Add the wine and simmer, scraping any brown bits off the base of the pan until reduced by half. Add the stock, return to a simmer, then return the chicken, skin side up, to the pan. Simmer until the chicken is cooked through. Add the asparagus and simmer for 2 minutes. Add the cream and tarragon and simmer until the asparagus is just tender.

ROASTED BACON-WRAPPED TURKEY WITH BRUSSELS SPROUTS & GRAVY

SERVES 4

2 garlic cloves, very finely chopped
grated zest of **1** large lemon
1 tablespoon thyme leaves, roughly chopped
sea salt and freshly ground black pepper
3 tablespoons olive oil
2 small boneless, skinless turkey breasts (about **800 g/1 lb 12 oz** total)
6 rashers (slices) smoked bacon, stretched thin
500 g (1 lb 2 oz) Brussels sprouts, trimmed and halved
1 tablespoon plain (all-purpose) flour
200 ml (7 fl oz) chicken or turkey stock

Preheat the oven to 200°C (400°F/Gas 6). Combine the garlic, lemon zest, thyme, ½ teaspoon each of salt and pepper and 2 tablespoons oil. Rub over the turkey. Arrange each turkey breast evenly on top of one another. Wrap the bacon around the turkey. Use string to tie the turkey into a cylindrical shape. Heat a large cast-iron skillet over medium heat and sear the turkey for 2 minutes on all sides. Roast in the oven for 20 minutes. Add Brussels sprouts to the pan, toss and season. Return to the oven and roast for 25 minutes until the sprouts are tender and the turkey registers 75°C (167°F) on a cooking thermometer. Remove the sprouts and keep warm if the turkey requires more cooking. Rest for 10 minutes, then slice. Return the pan to medium heat. Add the remaining oil, sprinkle over the flour and whisk to a paste. Gradually whisk in the stock and simmer for 1 minute before serving the gravy with turkey.

CHICKEN PICCATA

SERVES 4

4 small boneless, skinless chicken breasts, butterflied, cut in half and pounded to an even thickness
sea salt and freshly ground black pepper
50 g (2 oz/⅓ cup) plain (all-purpose) flour, for dusting
4 tablespoons olive oil
80 ml (2½ fl oz/⅓ cup) lemon juice plus **1** lemon, sliced
30 g (1 oz) unsalted butter, diced
100 ml (3½ fl oz/½ cup) chicken stock
3 tablespoons drained and rinsed capers
100 g (3½ oz) shelled broad beans or edamame, pods removed

Season the chicken and dust in flour. Heat a large stainless-steel skillet over medium–high heat. Add 2 tablespoons oil and cook half the chicken and lemon slices for 2–3 minutes per side (1 minute for the lemon) until brown. Remove and keep warm. Repeat with the remaining oil and chicken. Add 10 g (½ oz) butter to the pan and whisk in the lemon juice, stock and capers. Return the chicken to the pan and simmer for 5 minutes. Put the chicken on a plate and whisk the remaining butter into the sauce. Fold in the beans. Serve the sauce poured over the chicken.

ROAST CHICKEN WITH FENNEL & ONIONS

SERVES 4

1.5 kg (3 lb 5 oz) whole chicken
2 medium—large fennel bulbs, halved and sliced into 2 cm (¾ in) thick wedges
1 large red onion, halved and cut into 2 cm (¾ in) thick wedges
2 tablespoons olive oil, plus extra for rubbing
sea salt and freshly ground black pepper
1 lemon, halved crossways

Leave the chicken at room temperature for 1 hour. Preheat the oven to 200°C (400°F/Gas 6). Toss the fennel and onion with the oil, season and roast in a large skillet for 15 minutes. Remove from the oven, stir and add the lemon, cut sides down. Place the chicken on top, rub with oil and season. Roast for 1 hour, or until the juices run clear when a skewer is inserted in the thickest part of the meat. Squeeze the roasted lemon over the fennel, onion and sliced chicken.

SAUSAGE & WHITE BEAN CASSOULET

SERVES 4

1 tablespoon olive oil
8 best-quality sausages
450 g (1 lb) butternut squash, peeled and
  cut into 1 cm (½ in) pieces
4 oregano sprigs
2 garlic cloves, chopped
150 g (5 oz) cavolo nero, tough stems
  removed, leaves roughly chopped
1 x 400 g (14 oz) tin cannellini beans,
  drained and rinsed
sea salt and freshly ground black pepper
5 small tomatoes on the vine, halved

Preheat the oven 200°C (400°F/
Gas 6). Heat a large skillet over
medium—high heat, add the oil and
brown the sausages on all sides.
Remove from the pan. Add the squash
and oregano and cook for 5 minutes
until starting to colour. Add the
garlic and stir for 1 minute. Add
the cavolo nero and cook until
wilted. Add the beans, 200 ml
(7 fl oz) water, season and bring
to a simmer. Nestle in the tomatoes
and sausages and bake in the oven
for 25—30 minutes until the
sausages are cooked through and
the squash is tender.

COCONUT CHICKEN CURRY

SERVES 4

4 small boneless, skinless chicken breasts (about **550 g/1 lb 3 oz**), cut into small pieces
sea salt and freshly ground black pepper
1 tablespoon vegetable or coconut oil
1 small onion, chopped
2 tablespoons curry powder
3 garlic cloves, finely chopped
1 x 400 ml (13 fl oz) tin coconut milk
250 ml (8½ fl oz/1 cup) chicken stock
600 g (1 lb 5 oz) cooked basmati rice
1 small bunch of coriander (cilantro), leaves picked

Season the chicken. Heat a large skillet over medium—high heat. Add the oil and cook the chicken and onion for 8—10 minutes until golden brown. Add the curry powder and garlic and cook for 1 minute. Add the coconut milk and stock and bring to a simmer. Cook, covered, for 5 minutes until the chicken is cooked through. Fold in the rice and stir until hot. Sprinkle with the coriander.

ROASTED COQ AU VIN-STYLE CHICKEN

SERVES 4

100 g (3½ oz/⅔ cup) smoked bacon, cut into 1 cm (½ in)
   pieces
4 large shallots, peeled and quartered
8 small chicken thighs, fat and excess skin trimmed
4 tablespoons tomato purée (paste)
250 ml (8½ fl oz/1 cup) red wine
450 g (1 lb) small new potatoes (about 25 potatoes)
300 g (10½ oz) chestnut mushrooms, quartered
1 tablespoon chopped rosemary and thyme, plus extra
   thyme leaves to serve
sea salt and freshly ground black pepper

Preheat the oven to 220°C (430°F/Gas 7). Fry
the bacon in a large stainless-steel skillet
over medium heat for 8—10 minutes until crisp;
remove from the pan, leaving the fat behind.
Add the shallots and cook over medium—high
heat until golden brown, adding oil if
necessary. Remove from the pan. Season the
chicken and cook, skin side down, over medium
heat until golden brown. Turn and cook for
another 2 minutes. Remove from the pan and
keep warm. Add the tomato purée, stirring for
1 minute. Gradually stir in the wine. Bring
to a simmer, then add the potatoes, shallots,
bacon, mushrooms and herbs, tossing to coat.
Arrange in an even layer and return to a
simmer. Top with the chicken and roast for
30 minutes until the chicken is cooked.
Sprinkle with the thyme leaves.

QUICK BIRYANI

SERVES 4

200 g (7 oz/1 cup) basmati rice
3 tablespoons unsalted butter
1 onion, finely chopped
450 g (1 lb) lean minced (ground) lamb or beef
2 rounded tablespoons Indian curry paste
500 ml (17 fl oz/2 cups) chicken stock
1 large carrot, coarsely grated
10 g (½ oz) coriander (cilantro) leaves, chopped, plus
  leaves to garnish
lime wedges, to serve

Rinse the rice, soak for 10 minutes, then drain. Meanwhile, heat a large skillet over medium heat, add the butter and fry the onion for 10–12 minutes until starting to turn golden. Add the lamb and cook for 4–5 minutes until browned; drain any excess fat. Add the curry paste and cook, stirring, for 1 minute, then add the rice and stock. Simmer, covered, until the rice is tender. Fold in the carrot and chopped coriander. Garnish with extra coriander and serve with lime wedges.

POTATO, CHORIZO & EGG HASH

SERVES 4

175 g (6 oz) Spanish dried chorizo, peeled and sliced
2 tablespoons olive oil
1 red onion, chopped
3 potatoes (about **850 g/1 lb 14 oz**), peeled and cut into 1 cm (½ in) cubes
4 large eggs
50 g (2 oz) extra-mature Cheddar, grated

Preheat the oven to 190°C (375°F/ Gas 5). Cook the chorizo in a large cast-iron skillet over medium heat for 5 minutes until crisp. Transfer to a plate. Add the oil, onion and potatoes and cook, covered, for 10–15 minutes until the potatoes are tender. Return the chorizo to the pan, crack the eggs on top, sprinkle with cheese and bake in the oven for 10–14 minutes until the eggs are set.

TOAD IN THE HOLE

SERVES 4

6 large sausages
1 tablespoon oil
200 g (7 oz/1⅓ cups) plain (all-purpose) flour
sea salt and freshly ground black pepper
3 large eggs, at room temperature
400 ml (13 fl oz) whole milk, at room temperature
30 g (1 oz) unsalted butter, melted
1 tablespoon wholegrain mustard

Preheat the oven to 220°C (430°F/Gas 7).
Prick the sausages all over, transfer to
a large cast-ironskillet and toss with
the oil. Roast for 15 minutes. Whisk
together the flour and ¼ teaspoon each of
salt and pepper in a bowl. Make a well
in the flour, add the eggs and, while
whisking, gradually add the milk until
smooth. Add the butter and mustard. Pour
the batter around the sausages and bake
for 30—35 minutes until puffed and
golden.

BEEF & BROCCOLI STIR-FRY

SERVES 4

75 ml (2½ fl oz) soy sauce
1½ tablespoons brown sugar
20 g (¾ oz) piece of ginger, peeled and finely grated
2 garlic cloves, finely grated
1 small red chilli, thinly sliced
300 g (10½ oz) sirloin steak, thinly sliced
1 teaspoon cornflour (cornstarch)
2 tablespoons vegetable or coconut oil
1 broccoli crown (about **375 g/13 oz**), cut into small florets

Combine the soy, sugar, ginger, garlic and most of the chilli in a small bowl. Transfer half to a large bowl and toss with the steak. Marinate for 20 minutes or up to 1 day. Combine the cornflour and 2 teaspoons water in a small bowl. Whisk into the remaining soy mixture. Heat half the oil in a large skillet over medium—high heat and fry the beef for 3 minutes until cooked. Transfer to a plate. Add the remaining oil and cook the broccoli for 4 minutes. Return the steak to the pan, make a well in middle and add the sauce. Simmer, then toss with the broccoli and steak. Cook for 2 minutes, adding water, 1 tablespoon at a time, if the mixture looks dry or sticks. Top with the remaining chilli.

ROASTED PORK WITH PEARS & SHALLOTS

SERVES 4–6

900 g (2 lb) boneless pork loin, excess fat trimmed
sea salt and freshly ground black pepper
1 tablespoon finely chopped rosemary
2 garlic cloves
1 teaspoon coriander seeds
3 teaspoons olive oil
4 small pears, quartered and cored
4 small shallots, halved
125 ml (4 fl oz/½ cup) balsamic vinegar

Preheat the oven to 200°C (400°F/Gas 6).
Season the pork. Using a pestle and mortar,
pound the rosemary, garlic and coriander seeds
to a coarse paste. Add 2 teaspoons oil, mix
and rub all over the pork. Toss the pears and
shallots with the remaining oil and brown in
a large skillet over medium heat for 2 minutes
per side. Remove from the pan. Increase the
heat to medium–high and cook the pork for
4–5 minutes per side until brown. Remove from
the heat, add the vinegar, return the shallots
to the pan and roast in the oven for
20 minutes. Reduce the heat to 160°C (320°F/
Gas 3). Return the pears to the pan and
cook for 20 minutes until the pork registers
70°C (158°F) on a cooking thermometer. Rest
the pork for 10 minutes, then thinly slice.

SPICED BEEF HOT POT

SERVES 4–6

2 **tablespoons** olive oil
1 **kg (2 lb 3 oz)** lean chuck stew beef, cut into 6 cm
  (2½ in) pieces
sea salt and freshly ground black pepper
1 onion, sliced
3 carrots, cut on the diagonal into 10 cm (4 in) long
  pieces
2 **tablespoons** tomato purée (paste)
1 small cinnamon stick
125 ml (4 fl oz/½ cup) dry red wine
1 x **400 g (14 oz)** tin chopped tomatoes
1 **kg (2 lb 3 oz)** potatoes, peeled and cut into 1 cm
  (½ in) thick slices
2 **tablespoons** unsalted butter, melted

Preheat the oven to 160°C (320°F/Gas 3). Heat
1 tablespoon oil in a large stainless-steel
skillet over medium–high heat. Season the beef
with ½ teaspoon each of salt and pepper and,
working in batches, brown on all sides. Remove
from the pan, reduce the heat to low, add the
remaining oil and cook the onion and carrots
until starting to brown. Return the beef
to the pan, add the tomato purée and cook,
stirring, for 1 minute. Add the cinnamon and
wine and simmer, scraping any brown bits off
the base of the pan. Add the tomatoes, return
to a simmer then remove from the heat. Lay the
potatoes in a spiral, slightly overlapping,
brush with half the butter and sprinkle with
¼ teaspoon each of salt and pepper. Cover and
cook in the oven for 1½–1¾ hours until the
beef and potatoes are tender. Heat the grill
(broiler) to high. Brush the potatoes with the
rest of the butter and grill until golden.

CARNITAS WITH QUICK ONION PICKLE

SERVES 4

1.5 kg (3 lb 5 oz) boneless pork shoulder with a thin fat cap
sea salt and freshly ground black pepper
2 large garlic cloves, roughly chopped
4 poblano chillies, seeded and cut into large chunks
2 jalepeño chillies, halved, seeded and sliced
2 shallots, very thinly sliced
3 tablespoons lime juice
corn tortillas, to serve
hot sauce, to serve

Preheat the oven to 120°C (250°F/Gas ½). Lightly score the fat cap of the pork. Sprinkle ½ teaspoon salt over the garlic and use a knife to scrape into a paste. Rub all over the pork. Season with pepper. Transfer to a large cast-iron skillet, fat side up, and cook in the oven for 6–7 hours until the meat shreds easily. During the last 2 hours, place all the chillies on a sheet of foil, toss lightly with oil and bring the foil together to make a parcel. Place in the oven. Remove the pork and chillies from oven; remove the fat cap and shred the pork, discarding the fat, then chop the chillies and toss to combine. Increase the oven temperature to 220°C (430°F/Gas 7). Wipe out the skillet, return the fat cap to the pan and roast until crispy. Break the crackling into pieces. Toss the shallots in the lime juice and leave for 10 minutes or overnight, tossing occasionally. Serve with the pork, crackling, tortillas and hot sauce.

CREAMY MUSTARD PORK CHOPS

SERVES 4

4 boneless pork chops, (2 cm/¾ in thick), fat rind
  removed
sea salt and freshly ground black pepper
1 tablespoon unsalted butter
1 tablespoon olive oil
125 ml (4 fl oz/½ cup) dry cider
1 tablespoon wholegrain mustard
50 ml (2 fl oz) double (heavy) cream
1 bunch of mustard greens or curly kale, tough stems
  removed, leaves roughly chopped

Season the pork. Heat a large skillet over
medium–high heat. Add the butter and oil and,
once foaming, cook the pork for 5–7 minutes
per side until golden brown and cooked
through. Remove from the skillet and keep
warm. Add the cider to the pan and simmer,
scraping any brown bits off the base of the
pan. Reduce the heat to low, whisk in the
mustard and cream and simmer for 1 minute.
Season, then fold in the mustard greens
and serve with the pork.

LETTUCE CUPS WITH CRISPY THAI PORK

SERVES 2

2 tablespoons fish sauce
450 g (1 lb) minced (ground) pork
½ **tablespoon** vegetable oil
3 garlic cloves, finely chopped
20 g (¾ oz) piece of ginger, peeled and finely grated
1 red chilli, thinly sliced
4 tablespoons lime juice, plus **1 teaspoon** grated zest
1 handful each of mint and coriander (cilantro) leaves
25 g (1 oz) unsalted roasted peanuts, roughly chopped
2 baby gem lettuces, individual leaves separated,
   or **6** round lettuce leaves
lime wedges, to serve

Combine the fish sauce and pork and leave for 20 minutes. Heat a large skillet over medium—high heat, add the oil and cook the pork, breaking it into small pieces, for 10 minutes until crispy. Add the garlic, ginger and half the chilli, stirring for 1 minute. Remove from heat, add the lime juice and zest, herbs, the rest of the chilli and the peanuts. Serve in lettuce cups with lime wedges on the side.

SKILLET MEATBALLS

SERVES 4

1 large egg
30 g (1 oz) dried breadcrumbs
2 tablespoons each of chopped dill, mint
  and flat-leaf parsley, plus extra to serve
2 tablespoons lemon juice, plus **1 teaspoon**
  grated zest
6 large garlic cloves, (4 cloves thinly
  sliced; 2 left whole)
sea salt and freshly ground black pepper
450 g (1 lb) lean minced (ground) beef
  or bison
3 tablespoons olive oil
450 ml (15 fl oz) chicken stock
200 g (7 oz) shelled edamame
100 g (3½ oz) baby spinach

Beat the egg in a bowl. Add the
breadcrumbs, herbs and lemon zest
and grate in the two garlic cloves.
Add the beef, ½ teaspoon salt and
¼ teaspoon pepper and mix together.
Shape the mixture into meatballs.
Heat 1 tablespoon oil in a large
cast-iron skillet over medium–high
heat and brown the meatballs on
all sides. Remove and reduce the
heat to low. Add the remaining oil
and sliced garlic and cook until
starting to colour. Add the lemon
juice and stock, bring to a simmer,
then return the meatballs to
the pan. Cover and simmer for
25 minutes. Add the edamame and
return to a simmer. Fold in the
spinach until just wilted.

BEER-BRAISED SHORT RIBS

SERVES 4

4 boneless beef short ribs (English cut, about **900 g/2 lb**)
sea salt and freshly ground black pepper
2 tablespoons olive oil
1 large onion, roughly chopped
3 carrots (about **150 g/5 oz**), cut into 1 cm (½ in) pieces
3 tablespoons tomato purée (paste)
1 tablespoon chopped rosemary
350 ml (12 fl oz/1½ cups) dark ale
250 ml (8½ fl oz/1 cup) beef stock

Preheat the oven to 140°C (275°F/Gas 1). Season the ribs. Heat a
large skillet over medium—high heat. Add half the oil and brown
the ribs for 4 minutes per side. Remove from the pan and discard
the excess oil. Return the pan to medium heat, add the rest of the
oil and cook the onion and carrots for 5 minutes. Add the tomato
purée and cook for 1 minute. Add the rosemary, beer, stock and
150 ml (5 fl oz) water. Nestle the ribs in the pan and cover. Roast
for 2½–3 hours, turning once, until very tender.

SLOW-ROAST LAMB

SERVES 4—6

1 **tablespoon** finely chopped rosemary
4 anchovies
2 **teaspoons** grated lemon zest
4 garlic cloves, roughly chopped
1.5—1.8 kg (3 lb 5 oz—4 lb) semi-boneless
  leg of lamb, unrolled if tied up
sea salt and freshly ground black pepper
500 g (1 lb 5 oz) cherry or baby plum
  tomatoes
125 g (4½ oz) baby rocket
crusty bread, to serve

Preheat the oven to 150°C (300°F/
Gas 2). Using a pestle and mortar,
grind the rosemary, anchovies,
lemon zest and garlic to a coarse
paste. Season the lamb and cover in
the paste. Roll up, fat side up,
and transfer to a large cast-iron
skillet. Roast for 5½ hours until
the meat is very tender. During the
last 90 minutes of cooking, add the
tomatoes, tossing in the lamb fat.
Shred the lamb, discarding any fat
and return to the pan. Add the
rocket and toss to combine. Serve
with bread.

STEAK FAJITAS

SERVES 4

1 skirt steak, cut crossways into 3 pieces
3 tablespoons vegetable oil
sea salt and freshly ground black pepper
1 large red onion, sliced
2 green (bell) peppers, seeded and sliced
2 large garlic cloves, thinly sliced
1½ teaspoons ground cumin
200 g (7 oz) shop-bought guacamole, to serve
sour cream, to serve
4 medium flour tortillas, to serve

Heat a large skillet over medium–high heat.
Rub the steak with 1 tablespoon oil, season
and sear in the hot pan for 3–5 minutes per
side for medium-rare. Remove from the skillet,
reduce the heat to medium, add the remaining
oil and cook the onion and peppers for
10 minutes, tossing occasionally until tender.
Add the garlic and cumin, season and cook
for 1 minute. Slice the steak and serve
with the vegetables, guacamole, sour cream
and tortillas.

LAMB TAGINE

SERVES 4

900 g (2 lb) lamb stewing meat, fat
  trimmed, cut into 4 cm (1½ in) pieces
1 tablespoon ras el hanout
sea salt and freshly ground black pepper
3 tablespoons olive oil
1 large red onion, chopped
1 tablespoon tomato purée (tomato paste)
2 x 400 g (14 oz) tins whole plum tomatoes,
  crushed
1 x 400 g (14 oz) tin chickpeas
  (garbanzos), drained and rinsed
1 cinnamon stick
125 g (4 oz) dried apricots

Toss the lamb with the ras el
hanout and season. Heat a large
stainless-steel skillet over
medium—high heat. Add 2 tablespoons
oil and brown the lamb on all
sides. Transfer to a bowl. Reduce
the heat to low, add the remaining
oil and onion and cook, covered,
for 10 minutes. Uncover, add the
tomato purée and cook, stirring for
1 minute. Add the tomatoes, 250 ml
(8½ fl oz/1 cup) water, chickpeas,
cinnamon and apricots, and return
the lamb to the pan. Simmer gently,
covered, for 1½ hours until the
lamb is tender. Uncover and simmer
for 10—15 minutes until sauce
starts to thicken.

CAULIFLOWER CHEESE

SERVES 4

4 rashers (slices) streaky bacon
2 tablespoons unsalted butter
2½ tablespoons plain (all-purpose) flour
650 ml (22 fl oz) warm whole (full-fat) milk
1 small head cauliflower, tough stems
   discarded, cut into florets (about **750 g/
   1 lb 10 oz**)
200 g (7 oz) extra-mature Cheddar, grated
100 g (3½ oz) baby spinach
50 g (2 oz) Parmesan, finely grated

Preheat the oven to 180°C (350°F/
Gas 4). Cook the bacon in a large
skillet for 8–10 minutes until
crisp. Transfer to a plate lined
with kitchen paper to cool, then
roughly chop. Wipe out the pan.
Melt the butter until foaming,
sprinkle over the flour and whisk
for 1 minute until smooth. Gradually
whisk in the milk, stirring
continuously, and bring to the
boil. Add the cauliflower florets,
return to a simmer, then cover and
cook in the oven for 30–35 minutes
until tender, stirring once halfway
through. Fold in the Cheddar,
spinach and bacon. Heat the grill
(broiler) to high. Sprinkle the
Parmesan on top and grill until
light golden brown.

SKILLET

DECONSTRUCTED LASAGNE

SERVES 4

1 tablespoon olive oil
225 g (8 oz) sausages, casings removed
2 garlic cloves, finely chopped
1 small onion, finely chopped
500 ml (17 fl oz/2 cups) tomato (marinara) sauce
8 lasagne sheets (about **150 g/5 oz**), broken into small pieces
750 ml (25 fl oz/3 cups) chicken stock
sea salt and freshly ground black pepper
50 g (2 oz) cream cheese, at room temperature, cut into small pieces
100 g (3½ oz) mozzarella, sliced

Heat a large skillet over medium heat, add the oil, then the
sausage, garlic and onion and cook, breaking the sausage up
with the back of a spoon. Add the tomato sauce, pasta, stock
and seasoning and bring to the boil. Simmer vigorously, stirring
frequently with tongs for 16 minutes, or until the pasta is
tender. Remove from the heat. Heat the grill (broiler) to high.
Fold the cream cheese into the cooked pasta to melt, then top
with the mozzarella and grill until the cheese is bubbling.

SKILLET SPAGHETTI BOLOGNESE

SERVES 4

2 tablespoons olive oil
1 onion, finely chopped
1 carrot, finely chopped
450 g (1 lb) lean minced (ground) beef
2 tablespoons tomato purée (paste)
750 ml (25½ fl oz/3 cups) tomato (marinara) sauce
500 ml (17 fl oz/2 cups) chicken stock
325 g (11½ oz) dried spaghetti
sea salt and freshly ground black pepper
Parmesan shards, to serve

Heat a large stainless-steel skillet over medium heat, add the oil and cook the onion and carrot, covered, for 10 minutes, stirring occasionally, until very tender. Add the beef and cook until it is no longer pink. Drain any excess fat, then add the tomato purée, stirring for 1 minute. Add the tomato sauce, stock and pasta and simmer, turning the pasta until it softens and bends. Cover and simmer gently for 5 minutes, then uncover and cook for another 5 minutes until al dente. Season and serve with the Parmesan.

BEEF STROGANOFF

SERVES 4

2 tablespoons olive oil
275 g (9½ oz) chestnut mushrooms, stems
   trimmed and sliced
sea salt and freshly ground black pepper
450 g (1 lb) lean sirloin, thinly sliced
2 garlic cloves, finely chopped
2 tablespoons Dijon mustard
125 ml (4 fl oz/½ cup) dry white wine
850 ml (28½ fl oz) beef stock
200 g (7 oz) fusilli
3 tablespoons crème fraîche

Heat a large skillet over medium–
high heat. Add 1 tablespoon oil and
fry the mushrooms for 5 minutes,
seasoning as they cook, or until
browned. Transfer to a bowl. Return
the pan to medium heat, add the
remaining oil, season the beef and
cook until no longer pink. Add the
garlic and stir for 1 minute. Next,
stir in the mustard to coat. Add
the wine, scrape any brown bits
from the base of the pan, then pour
in the stock and bring to a simmer.
Add the pasta, reserved mushrooms
(and juices) and simmer, stirring,
until the pasta is al dente. Add
the crème fraîche and season to
taste.

LEMON CHICKEN TORTELLINI

SERVES 4

350 g (12 oz) boneless, skinless chicken breast, cut into 2 cm (¾ in) pieces
sea salt and freshly ground black pepper
1½ tablespoons extra-virgin olive oil
2 garlic cloves, finely chopped
500 ml (17 fl oz/2 cups) chicken or vegetable stock
350 g (12 oz) small fresh cheese tortellini
225 g (8 oz) sugar snap peas, trimmed, halved on the diagonal
50 g (2 oz) cream cheese
2 tablespoons lemon juice

Season the chicken. Heat a large skillet over medium heat, add the oil and cook the chicken for 6–8 minutes until golden brown and cooked through. Remove from the pan and keep warm. Add the garlic and cook until starting to turn golden. Add the stock and bring to a simmer. Add the tortellini, simmer for 4–7 minutes, stirring, until cooked according to the packet instructions. Add the sugar snaps during the last 3 minutes of cooking. Remove the pan from the heat, whisk in the cheese, then add the lemon juice. Return the chicken to the pan and season with pepper to serve.

BAKED ORZO & LAMB CHOPS

SERVES 4

2 **tablespoons** olive oil
2 **tablespoons** capers, drained, rinsed and patted dry
1 **tablespoon** lemon juice and **2 teaspoons** zest (peeled and thinly sliced)
1 **tablespoon** finely chopped flat-leaf parsley
salt and freshly ground black pepper
8 lamb loin chops, fat trimmed
125 ml (4 fl oz/½ cup) dry white wine
225 g (8 oz) orzo
500 ml (17 fl oz/2 cups) chicken stock
25 g (1 oz) Parmesan, finely grated

Preheat the oven to 200°C (400°F/Gas 6). Heat a large skillet over medium heat. Add the oil and fry the capers until crisp. Remove from the pan and, once cool, toss with the lemon zest and parsley in a bowl. Season the lamb. Increase the heat to medium—high and cook the lamb for 2–3 minutes per side until golden brown; remove and keep warm. Drain the fat from the pan, add the wine and cook for 1 minute, scraping any brown bits off the base of the pan. Add the orzo and toss to coat. Add the stock and bring to a simmer. Cook in the oven for 8 minutes, then remove and nestle the lamb into the orzo. Return to the oven until the orzo is tender and nearly all the liquid has been absorbed; remove the lamb and fold in the lemon juice and Parmesan. Serve with the lamb and capers.

MAC & CHEESE

SERVES 4

4 tablespoons unsalted butter, cut into
small pieces
4 tablespoons plain (all-purpose) flour
sea salt and freshly ground black pepper
750 ml (25½ fl oz/3 cups) warm whole milk
225 g (8 oz) lumache, cavatappi or small
pasta shells
225 g (8 oz) mature Cheddar, coarsely
grated
2 tablespoons finely grated Parmesan

Preheat the oven to 180°C (350°F/
Gas 4). Melt the butter in a large
skillet over medium heat. Once
foaming, add the flour and whisk
until smooth. Gradually whisk in
the milk. Add 250 ml (8½ fl oz/
1 cup) water, ½ teaspoon each of
salt and pepper and bring to a
simmer, stirring occasionally.
Immediately add the pasta and cook,
stirring for 1 minute. Cover and
bake in the oven for 12–14 minutes
until the pasta is just cooked.
Remove from the oven and fold the
cheese into the pasta until melted
and smooth.

THREE CHEESE CANNELLONI

SERVES 4

1 tablespoon olive oil
1 large onion, halved and finely chopped
300 g (10½ oz) whole milk ricotta
110 g (4 oz) mozzarella
50 g (2 oz) grated Parmesan
1 large egg
10 g (½ oz) basil leaves, roughly chopped
salt and freshly ground black pepper
550 ml (17 fl oz/2 cups) tomato (marinara) sauce
250 g (9 oz) fresh lasagne sheets

Preheat the oven to 190°C (375°F/Gas 5). Heat a
large stainless-steel skillet over medium—low heat.
Add the oil and fry the onion until starting to
colour. Transfer to a bowl. Meanwhile, combine the
cheeses, egg and basil and season. Pour 400 ml
(13 fl oz) tomato sauce into the base of the pan.
Cut the lasagne sheets into 15 x 10 cm (6 x 4 in)
strips. Working one at a time, place 4 tablespoons
of mixture at the short end of each pasta sheet and
roll up. Arrange, seam side down, in the sauce.
Spoon the remaining sauce on top, then scatter with
onion and cheese. Bake for 25—30 minutes until
bubbling and starting to turn golden.

RAVIOLI WITH HARISSA & BASIL

SERVES 2

1 tablespoon olive oil
3 garlic cloves, thinly sliced
300 ml (10 fl oz) chicken stock
300 g (10½ oz) packet of cheese or mushroom
   ravioli
100 g (3½ oz) mild harissa
50 g (2 oz) labneh
basil leaves, for sprinkling

Heat a large skillet over medium heat. Add the oil and fry the garlic until golden. Transfer to a plate. Add the stock and ravioli to the pan and simmer gently, stirring and turning occasionally until cooked according to the instructions on the packet. Add the harissa and garlic. Remove from the heat and whisk in the labneh until melted. Sprinkle with basil.

PASTA PRIMAVERA

SERVES 4

225 g (8 oz) fusilli or penne pasta
  (cooking time between 7–9 minutes)
750 ml (25½ fl oz/3 cups) hot chicken or
  vegetable stock
250 g (8 oz) medium-thin asparagus, woody
  stems discarded, stalks cut into 3 cm
  (1¼ in) pieces
1 small bunch of broccolini (about **225 g/
  8 oz**), ends trimmed, larger stalks halved
125 g (4 oz) peas, thawed if frozen
3 tablespoons crème fraîche or cream
50 g (2 oz/½ cup) Parmesan, finely grated
1 tablespoon chopped tarragon
sea salt and freshly ground black pepper

Place the pasta in a large skillet
and pour over the hot stock. Bring
to the boil, then simmer for
5 minutes, stirring. Add the
asparagus and broccolini, boil,
then cover and simmer for 5 minutes.
Uncover and check the pasta. Simmer
for another minute if needed, until
al dente. Remove from the heat, add
the peas, crème fraîche, Parmesan
and tarragon. Season to taste.

UPSIDE-DOWN BANANA CAKE

SERVES 8–10

6 ripe bananas
110 g (4 oz) unsalted butter
225 g (8 oz) soft brown sugar
100 g (4 oz) granulated sugar
3 large eggs
1 teaspoon pure vanilla extract
250 g (9 oz/1⅔ cups) plain (all-purpose) flour
2 teaspoons baking powder (soda)
½ teaspoon salt

Preheat the oven to 180°C (350°F/Gas 4). Mash 3 bananas in a large bowl. Melt the butter in a 23 cm (9 in) cast-iron skillet over medium heat until golden. Remove from the heat, transfer the butter to the bowl with the bananas. Sprinkle 150 g (5 oz) brown sugar evenly over the base of the skillet. Slice the remaining bananas in half lengthways and arrange in a single layer, cut side down, on top of the sugar. Add the remaining sugars, eggs and vanilla extract to the bananas. Sift over the flour, baking powder and the salt; fold to combine. Pour over the bananas, place a piece of foil on an oven rack, put the skillet on top and bake for 40–45 minutes until a skewer inserted in the middle comes out clean. Leave to stand for 5 minutes, then invert onto a serving plate.

BERRY CRUMBLE

SERVES 4–6

350 g (12 oz) raspberries
150 g (5 oz) blueberries
1 tablespoon cornflour (cornstarch)
80 g (3 oz) caster (superfine) sugar
100 g (3½ oz) unsalted butter, cubed
125 g (4 oz) plain (all-purpose) flour
25 g (1 oz) rolled oats

Preheat the oven to 190°C (375°F/
Gas 5). Toss together the berries,
cornflour and 2 tablespoons sugar,
then transfer to a 23 cm (9 in)
cast-iron skillet. Rub the butter
into the flour in a bowl until it
resembles breadcrumbs. Add the
remaining sugar and oats and squeeze
into small clumps. Scatter over the
berries and bake for 35–40 minutes
until the berries are bubbling and
the topping is golden.

GOOEY BROWNIES

SERVES 8—10

175 g (6 oz) good-quality dark chocolate, finely chopped
150 g (5 oz) unsalted butter, cut into small pieces
3 large eggs
200 g (7 oz) golden caster (superfine) sugar
75 g (2½ oz) ground hazelnuts or almonds
50 g (2 oz) good-quality cocoa powder
pinch of salt

Preheat the oven to 180°C (350°F/Gas 4). Place
an oven rack in the lower third of the oven.
Microwave the chocolate and butter together in
a large bowl until melted. Using an electric
whisk, whisk the eggs and sugar to combine.
Add the melted chocolate and mix gently to
combine. Fold in the ground hazelnuts, cocoa
powder and salt. Transfer to a 23 cm (9 in)
cast-iron skillet and bake for 25 minutes.

DUTCH BABY WITH LEMON SUGAR & BLUEBERRIES

SERVES 4–6

4 large eggs
250 ml (8½ fl oz/1 cup) warm whole (full-fat) milk
125 g (4 oz) plain (all-purpose) flour
50 g (2 oz) granulated sugar, plus **1 tablespoon**
1 teaspoon pure vanilla extract
pinch of salt
3 tablespoons unsalted butter
1 teaspoon grated lemon zest
175 g (6 oz) blueberries

Preheat the oven to 220°C (430°F/Gas 7). Heat a large cast-iron skillet over medium heat. In a blender, combine the eggs, milk, flour, 50 g (2 oz) sugar, vanilla extract and salt, scraping down the sides if necessary. Heat the butter in the hot skillet until foamy. Transfer the batter to the pan and bake in the oven for 20 minutes until puffed and golden. Rub the remaining sugar and lemon zest between your fingers to combine. Scatter the sugar mix over the Dutch baby, along with the blueberries.

CRÊPES

MAKES 8

4 large eggs
250 ml (8½ fl oz/1 cup) whole milk
120 g (4½ oz) plain (all-purpose) flour
1 tablespoon caster (superfine) sugar
pinch of salt
coconut oil, for frying

Combine the eggs, milk, flour, sugar and salt
in a blender and purée for 15 seconds, scraping
down the sides once. Chill for 30 minutes or
up to 48 hours. Heat a large stainless-steel
skillet over medium heat. Add ½ teaspoon
coconut oil, swirling to coat the base of the
pan. Add 75 ml (2½ fl oz) batter, immediately
swirling the pan to coat. Cook for 45 seconds
until light golden brown. Flip and cook for
another 30 seconds. Remove from the skillet
and repeat until all the batter has been used.

CHERRY CLAFOUTIS

SERVES 6

1 tablespoon unsalted butter
200 ml (7 fl oz) whole milk
50 ml (2 fl oz) double (heavy) cream
3 large eggs
60 g (2 oz) plain (all-purpose) flour
1 teaspoon pure vanilla paste
100 g (3½ oz) granulated sugar,
   plus **2 tablespoons**
350 g (12 oz/1¾ cups) cherries, stoned

Preheat the oven to 180°C (350°F/
Gas 4). Melt the butter in a large
cast-iron skillet over medium heat
until foaming. Purée the milk,
cream, eggs, flour, vanilla paste and
100 g (3½ oz) sugar in a blender
until smooth. Transfer to the pan,
scatter over the cherries and bake
for 40—45 minutes until golden.
Sprinkle with the remaining sugar.

RASPBERRY ALMOND SCONE

SERVES 6—8

250 g (9 oz/1⅔ cups) plain (all-purpose) flour
2 teaspoons baking powder
pinch of sea salt
4 tablespoons golden caster (superfine) sugar,
 plus **2 teaspoons**
85 g (3 oz) coconut oil, melted
½ teaspoon pure almond extract
65 ml (2¼ fl oz) hot water
150 g (5 oz) raspberries
25 g (1 oz/¼ cup) flaked almonds

Preheat the oven to 180°C (350°F/Gas 4).
Place a rack in the lower third of the oven.
Combine the flour, baking powder, salt and
4 tablespoons sugar in a bowl. In another
bowl, combine the oil and almond extract.
Using a fork to stir, add to the flour mixture
to create small clumps. Add the hot water,
then the raspberries, folding together. Bring
together into a ball without overworking
the mixture and transfer to a 23 cm (9 in)
cast-iron skillet. Sprinkle with the almonds
and remaining sugar. Bake in the oven for
40—50 minutes until golden and a skewer
inserted into the middle comes out clean.

CHOCOLATE CHIP COOKIE

MAKES 1 X 23 CM (9 IN) COOKIE

100 g (3½ oz) coconut sugar
75 g (2½ oz/⅓ cup) granulated sugar
100 g (3½ oz) unsalted butter, at room temperature
½ teaspoon sea salt, plus **¼ teaspoon** sea salt flakes
1 large egg
1 teaspoon pure vanilla paste
100 g (3½ oz/⅔ cup) plain (all-purpose) flour
¼ teaspoon bicarbonate of soda (baking soda)
130 g (4½ oz) dark chocolate, roughly chopped

Preheat the oven to 190°C (375°F/Gas 5). Place a rack on the lowest position in the oven. Combine the sugars, butter and ½ teaspoon salt until smooth. Mix in the egg and vanilla paste. Add the flour and bicarbonate of soda and mix until a dough forms. Fold in three-quarters of the chocolate. Transfer the dough to a 23 cm (9 in) cast-iron or stainless-steel (greased) skillet and pat the dough to the edges of the pan. Scatter over the remaining chocolate and sprinkle with the remaining salt. Bake for 22–27 minutes until just set in the centre. Leave to cool for 1 hour before serving.

APPLE & ALMOND PUDDING CAKE

SERVES 6–8

10 g (½ oz) unsalted butter, melted
  plus extra for greasing
100 g (3½ oz/1 cup) ground almonds
¼ teaspoon salt
2 large eggs
175 g (6 oz/¾ cup) caster (superfine)
  sugar
1 teaspoon pure almond extract
1 large green apple, peeled and cored
25 g (1 oz/¼ cup) flaked almonds

Preheat the oven to 180°C (350°F/ Gas 4). Grease a 23 cm (9 in) cast-iron skillet with butter. Combine the ground almonds and salt in a large bowl. In another bowl, beat the eggs and all but 1 tablespoon sugar until pale and thick. Whisk in the almond extract, then fold in the dry ingredients. Chop half of the apple (thinly slice the remaining half and set aside) and fold in. Transfer the mixture to the skillet. Arrange the remaining sliced apple on top of the batter. Brush with the melted butter, sprinkle over the almonds and remaining sugar. Bake for 40–45 minutes until the top is golden brown.

PEAR TARTE TATIN

SERVES 6–8

150 g (5 oz/⅔ cup) caster (superfine) sugar
45 g (1½ oz) unsalted butter, cubed
pinch of coarse sea salt
7 small ripe but firm pears (about **900 g/2 lb** total),
  peeled, halved and cored
100 g (5 oz) marzipan (almond paste)
300 g (10½ oz) pre-rolled puff pastry, trimmed into
  a 24 cm (9½ in) circle (5 mm/¼ in thick)

Preheat the oven to 200°C (400°F/Gas 6). Heat
a large stainless-steel skillet over medium–
high heat. Add the sugar and cook, shaking the
pan, until a deep amber colour. Remove from
the heat and add the butter and salt. Arrange
the pears in the pan, cut side up, and return
to the heat for 10–12 minutes until nearly
tender and caramelised, turning occasionally.
Turn the pears cut side up and dot the cores
with pieces of marzipan. Drape the pastry over
the pears, pushing the excess inside the pan.
Bake for 30 minutes until golden. Leave to
rest for 5 minutes, then invert onto a plate.

CHOCOLATE SWIRL ROLLS

MAKES 12

125 ml (4 fl oz/½ cup) milk plus
  2 tablespoons, at room temperature
125 ml (4 fl oz/½ cup) warm water
2 teaspoons fast-action dried yeast
2 tablespoons caster (superfine) sugar
375 g (13 oz/2½ cups) plain (all-purpose)
  flour, plus extra for dusting
100 g (3½ oz) unsalted butter, melted,
  plus **1 tablespoon**
50 g (2 oz) good-quality dark chocolate
125 g (4 oz/1 cup) icing (confectioner's)
  sugar
1 tablespoon good-quality cocoa powder
sea salt

Combine 125 ml (4 fl oz/½ cup) milk
with water. Add the yeast, sugar
and 125 g (4 oz) flour and mix to
combine. Set aside for 10 minutes
until bubbling. Mix in 50 g (2 oz)
melted butter, ½ teaspoon salt and
the remaining flour to make a dough.
Cover and leave in a warm place for
1 hour, or until doubled in size.
Meanwhile, melt the chocolate with
50 g (2 oz) butter. Sift the icing
sugar and cocoa into a bowl and
stir to combine. On a lightly
floured surface, roll the dough into
a 23 x 30 cm (9 x 12 in) rectangle.
Spread with the chocolate mixture
and, starting at the long end, roll
the dough up tightly. Cut into
12 rolls and transfer to a large
cast-iron skillet. Cover and let
rise for 1 hour. Preheat the oven
to 180°C (350°F/Gas 4). Bake for
25—27 minutes until golden brown.
Melt the remaining icing sugar,
milk and butter in a small pan,
then drizzle over the hot rolls.

Thank you the wonderful Catie Ziller, Kathy Steer and Alice Chadwick for all their amazing work on this book and always. Thank you also to Beatriz da Costa and Frances Boswell for the incredible pictures and food styling.

To my mum, who always likes to get the washing up done before dinner — this one's for you! To my dad who likes to avoid the washing up, here's a great excuse!

To my Don, Charlie and Poppy — you guys are my everything.

First published by © Hachette Livre (Marabout) 2017
The English language edition published in 2018 by Hardie Grant Books,
an imprint of Hardie Grant Publishing

Hardie Grant Books (London)
5th & 6th Floors
52—54 Southwark Street
London SE1 1UN

Hardie Grant Books (Melbourne)
Building 1, 658 Church Street
Richmond, Victoria 3121

hardiegrantbooks.com

Text © Anna Helm Baxter 2018
Photography © Beatriz Da Costa 2018

British Library Cataloguing-in-Publication Data. A catalogue record for this book is available from the British Library.

Skillet by Anna Helm Baxter

ISBN 978-1-78488-156-6

Publisher: Catie Ziller
Photography: Beatriz Da Costa
Food Stylist: Frances Boswell
Designer and illustrator: Alice Chadwick
Editor: Kathy Steer

For the English hardback edition:

Publisher: Kate Pollard
Publishing Assistant: Eila Purvis
Editor: Andrea O'Connor
Proofreader: Delphine Phin

Colour Reproduction by p2d
Printed and bound in China by 1010